Herbert Howells

SIR PATRICK SPENS
Op. 23

for baritone solo, SATB chorus and orchestra

Vocal score

Herbert Howells first set the Scottish ballad *Sir Patrick Spens* for baritone solo, choir and orchestra in 1917. The vocal score was published in 1928 and manuscripts of the full score have survived at the Royal College of Music, London and the Bodleian Library, Oxford. The work went unheard for over sixty years and any performing materials were lost until the full score and parts were newly engraved for a performance in 2006 by the Bach Choir of London conducted by David Hill.

A second version of the work written by Howells in 1919 for four solo voices, string quartet and piano has not survived.

NOVELLO
Novello Publishing Limited (part of the Music Sales Group)
14/15 Berners Street, London W1T 3LJ, England
Exclusive distibutors: Music Sales Limited,
Newmarket Road, Bury St Edmunds, Suffolk IP33 3YB
Order No. NOV956549
www.chesternovello.com

To
Sir William S. McCormick

SIR PATRICK SPENS

HERBERT HOWELLS
Op. 23

6

The King's daugh-ter of Nor - ro-way

rall. Tempo, come prima

'Tis we must bring her hame."

(colla parte) *ff*

rit. - al - -

⑧ *più moderato*

12

14

15

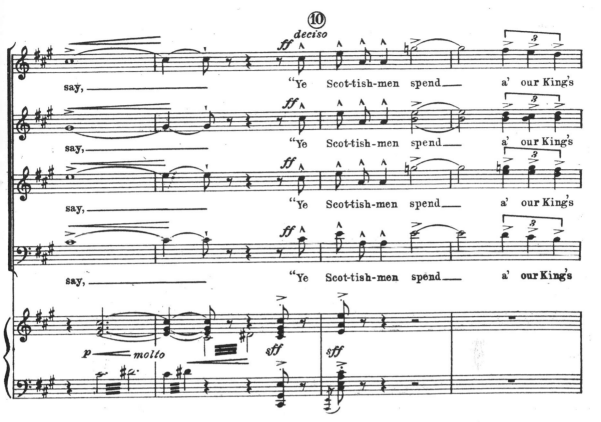

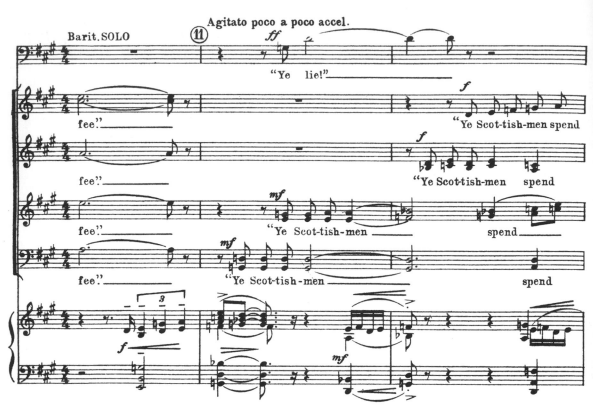

18

cres - - cen - . - - do - - - -
men and me; And I ha'e brought a half
hear ye lie! For we ha'e brought a half
hear ye lie! For we ha'e brought a half
hear ye lie! For we ha'e brought a half fou' o'
hear ye lie! For we ha'e half fou' o'
fff
fou' o' gude red goud out o'er the sea wi'
fou' o' gude red goud, Out o'er the sea
fou' o' gude red goud, Out o'er the sea
gude red goud, Out o'er the sea
gude red goud, Out o'er the sea

20

21

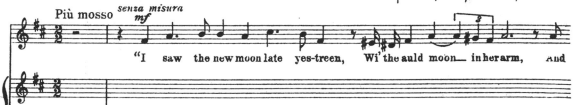

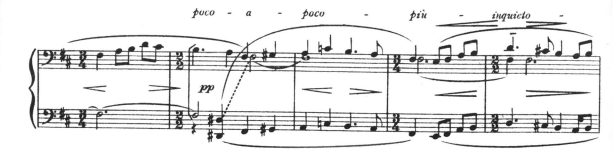

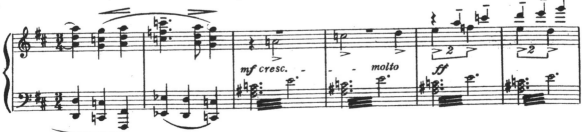

24

26

28

(19) Baritone Solo. *f*

"O where will I get a gude___ sail - or To take the helm in___ hand Till I___ get up to the tall top - mast To

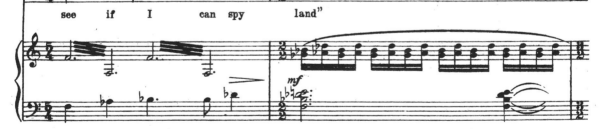

A Tenor voice.

Baritone Solo.

see if I can spy land" "O here am

I, a sail - or bold, To take the helm in hand, Till you get up to the

40

42

*Note:— If the chorus contain among it a capable Soloist, it will be best if she sings the 1st Soprano part to sign ⊕

44

46

48

Pat-rick Spens, Wi' the Scots lords at his

Pat-rick Spens, Wi' the Scots lords at his

Pat-rick Spens, Wi' the Scots lords at his

Pat-rick Spens, Wi' the Scots lords at his

a tempo, ma meno mosso.

feet.

feet.

feet.

feet.